GO LIVE!

THE JOKE BOX JOKE BOOK

EDITED AND COMPILED BY
CHRIS BELLINGER AND CATHY GILBEY
with cartoons
by Ian Dicks

BBC BOOKS

Published by BBC Books,
a division of BBC Enterprises Limited,
Woodlands, 80 Wood Lane, London W12 0TT
First Published 1988

© BBC Books 1988
Illustrations © Ian Dicks
ISBN 0 563 20711 6

Set in Univers Medium 10 on 12 point
Typeset by Phoenix Photosetting, Chatham
Printed and bound in Great Britain by
Richard Clay Ltd, Bungay, Suffolk
Cover printed by Fletchers of Norwich

CONTENTS

FOREWORD

When we asked 'what makes you laugh?' you
certainly told us!
Viewers of BBC TV's top Saturday morning
magazine show *Going Live!* wrote to us with jokes
galore. There are some old ones and some new
ones but you can be sure that every single one got
a high score on the *Going Live!* joke-ometer.
Thanks to everyone who sent them and
congratulations if we printed yours. Thanks too to
Cathy Speight who designed the book and Shona
Murray who helped co-ordinate it. We hope you
enjoy it . . .

JUST FOR STARTERS

What is the most important thing to remember in Chemistry?
Never lick the spoon.

BOY: Dad I need a new pair of plimsolls for gym.

DAD: Let Jim buy his own plimsolls.

SUSAN:	Have you said your prayers?
LITTLE BROTHER:	Yes, and I asked for something special.
SUSAN:	What was that?
LITTLE BROTHER:	I asked God to make Rome the capital of France.
SUSAN:	Why did you do that?
LITTLE BROTHER:	Because that's what I put in my Geography test today.

What do you call a television presenter that walks into the studio door?
Stupid.

Why did the dinosaur cross the road?
Because there weren't any chickens in those days.

Why did the gingerbread man wear trousers?
Because he had crumby legs.

MUM: Cynthia, please go outside to play your mouth organ – your father can't read the paper.
CYNTHIA: Huh – I'm only six and I can read it.

Did you hear about the lady who wanted something with diamonds in it?
Her husband bought her a pack of cards.

What has eight legs and gives milk?
Four milkmen – or two cows.

If a green stone fell into the Red Sea what would happen?
It would sink.

MUM: What did your Dad say when he saw your school report?
BOY: Shall I leave out the bad language?
MUM: Of course.
BOY: He didn't say a word.

Why did the hedgehog have dandruff?
Because he left his head and shoulders by the road.

What did the drill say to the hammer?
I've got such a boring job.

The three bears came home from an all-night disco. Daddy bear said, 'Who's been eating my porridge?', Mummy bear said, 'Who's been eating my porridge?' And Baby bear said, 'Never mind the porridge – who's stolen the video?'

Why did the bubble gum cross the road?
It was stuck to the chicken's foot.

There was a Welshman, an Englishman and a nun playing darts. The Englishman threw first and the Master of Ceremonies cried out 'One hundred and twenty'. The nun threw next and the Master of Ceremonies cried out 'One hundred and sixty'. The Welshman threw next but the nun didn't get out of the way in time, so the Master of Ceremonies called out 'One nun dead and eighty'.

What did Bruce Forsyth say to Dennis Taylor?
Good frame, good frame, good frame.

Why didn't the skeleton cross the road?
Because he hadn't any guts.

Why is a plumber like a Scottish musician?
Because they are both expert with the pipes.

Why shouldn't we eat pancakes?
Because eating pans is very bad for your teeth.

How did Little Bo Peep lose her sheep?
She had a crook with her.

What did the pilot say when he kissed his wife and left for work?
Ta-ta, love . . . must fly now.

A mouse went into a music shop.
'Have you got a mouse organ please?' he said.
'That's funny', said the assistant, 'you're the second mouse we've had in here today'.
'Must have been our Monica.'

A man was walking in the park when he found a penguin. He picked it up and took it to a policeman and said, 'I've found this penguin, what should I do?'

'Take it to the zoo', said the policeman.

The next day the policeman saw the man walking through the town centre with the penguin beside him.

'Didn't I tell you to take that creature to the zoo?' said the policeman.

'Yes', replied the man, 'that's what I did yesterday, today I'm taking him to the pictures.'

What do you call a lady who throws all her bills on the fire?
Bernadette.

MAN IN RIVER: Help, I can't swim!
PASSER BY: So what, I can't play the piano but I don't go shouting about it.

'Waiter, waiter what do you call this?'
'Bean salad, sir.'
'I don't care what it has been, what is it now?'

Why did the boy have Egyptian flu?
He caught it from his mummy.

HELEN: Mum, do you know what I'm going to give you for your birthday?
MUM: No dear, what?
HELEN: A nice teapot
MUM: But I've got a nice teapot.
HELEN: No you haven't. I've just dropped it.

'Doctor, if this swelling on my legs gets any bigger I won't be able to get my trousers on'.
'Then you better take this'.
'What is it?'
'The address of a nudist colony'.

A customer was sitting in a restaurant. He had just finished his meal when the waiter brought the bill. It read: OMELETE   £1.25
                TEA   40p
'Take this back', said the customer to the waiter 'and write it again so that it reads – omelette, with two t's.'
A few minutes later the waiter returned with a new bill and it read:
            OMELETE   £1.25
            2 TEAS   80p

How did the dinner-lady get a shock?
She stood on a bun and a currant went up her leg.

'Doctor, Doctor, I think I need glasses.'
'Man – so do I, you're in the pet shop.'

What did the mother glow-worm say to the father glow-worm?
Isn't our son bright for his age.

There was an Englishman, an Irishman and a Chinaman in an aeroplane. The Englishman said, 'There's a piece of England.' The Irishman said, 'There's a piece of Ireland', and the Chinaman dropped his coffee cup and said, 'There's a piece of China.'

A lady asked her daughter what was the minimum depth of a water polo pool.
The daughter's reply was 10 feet.
'Don't be so silly', retorted her mother, 'it must be shallower than that otherwise the horses would drown.'

What's brown, hangs on trees and can't sing?
Des O'Conker.

An Australian was showing a Texan around his farm, and he pointed proudly to his cows.
'Why that's nothing', said the Texan, 'Back home we have pigs as big as those cows.' The Australian then showed him his sheep. 'Why,' said the Texan, 'back home we have cats that are bigger than those sheep.'
At that moment a kangaroo came hopping by.
'Say,' said the Texan, impressed at last, 'You sure have fine grasshoppers out here.'

'Doctor, Doctor, my wife thinks she's a duck'.
'Bring her to see me tomorrow'
'I can't – she's just flown south for the winter.'

Did you hear about the plastic surgeon who stood by the fire?
He melted.

What does an Australian call an Englishman who's had a little too much to drink?
A tiddley pom.

What's the difference between a well-dressed man and a tired dog?
One wears a suit and the other 'just pants'.

There were two eggs in a saucepan and one egg turned to his friend and said,
'My goodness, it's hot in here isn't it?'
And the other egg said,
'Yes, but just wait till you get out, it's even worse, you get your head bashed in.'

There was a tomato and an egg sitting in a frying
pan. The egg said 'Gosh, isn't it hot in here?'
What do you think the tomato replied?
'Oh my goodness – a talking egg!'

A baby polar bear went up to his mum and said,

POLAR BEAR: Eh Mum, are you sure I'm a polar
bear, not a koala or a grizzly or
something?

MUM: Yes son, you're definitely a polar
bear.

So the polar bear went to his dad and said,

POLAR BEAR: Eh Dad, are you sure I'm a polar
bear, not a koala or a grizzly or
something?

DAD: Yes lad, you're *definitely* a
polar bear.

So he went to his Grandad and said,

POLAR BEAR: Grandad, are you *sure* I'm a polar
bear, not a koala or a grizzly or
something?

GRANDAD: Yes boy, you're *definitely* a polar
bear. Why do you ask?

POLAR BEAR: Cos I'm cold!

'TOP OF THE FLOPS'

What did **Madonna** say when she met a bear who had too much to drink?
He's like a FUR-GIN.

What did **George Michael** say to his illuminated alarm clock?
Wake me up before you GLO GLO.

What did **A-Ha** say when they saw the forest fire?
FRY WOLF.

What did **Boy George** say when he was an animal tamer in the circus?
Camel, camel, camel, camel, camel, CAMEL-LION.

What did **Michael Jackson** say when he reverted to childhood?
I'm sounding SHRILLER.

What did **Tiffany** say at the end of a long journey?
I think we're AT HOME now.

What did **Diana Ross** say when British Rail went on strike?
I'm in the middle of a TRAIN INACTION.

What did the teacher say when the **Beatles** told a naughty joke?
Hey RUDE.

What did **T'Pau** say when they found a tea-set at the bottom of the garden?
China in my LAND.

What did **Rick Astley** say when he gave up his job on the building site?
Never going to TIP A TRUCK.

What did **Shakin' Stevens** say when he'd finished spring cleaning?
CLEAN FLOOR.

What did **The Police** say when the new puppy had an accident on the floor?
Every MESS you make.

What did **Bonnie Tyler** say when her record reached number 1?
TOTAL BLITZ on the Charts.

What did **Pink Floyd** say when their beach-ball burst?
Just Another NICK IN THE BALL.

What did **Sinitta** say when she met Michael Jackson?
Oh JACKO.

What did **Kylie Minogue** *say when she fell in the gunge tank?*
I should be so MUCKY.

What did **5 Star** say when asked what they wanted to play at a Christmas party?
This 5 say CHESS.

What did **Annie Lennox** say when she bought some velcro?
NEAT SEAMS are made of this.

'BACK TO BUSINESS'

How do you keep a *Going Live!* viewer in suspense?
I'll tell you tomorrow.

'Doctor, Doctor I think I'm a hi-fi system.'
'Well, you certainly are a loud speaker.'

JUDGE: Why did you steal all those 5p, 10p, 20p and 50p pieces?
DEFENDANT: Well, sir, I wasn't feeling well and I thought the change would be good for me.

What do you call a brother and sister with food poisoning?
Sam 'n' Ella.

James and Peter were walking down the road when Peter fell over and couldn't get up.
JAMES: What should I do?
PETER: Call me an ambulance, I think I've broken my leg.
JAMES: Peter is an ambulance, Peter is an ambulance.

How did the woodwork teacher break his teeth?
He bit his nails.

Why did Michael Jackson call his album 'Bad'?
Because he couldn't spell DIABOLICAL.

A lady on a crowded bus missed her stop and started to shout at the conductor, 'Hey I've missed my stop.'
The bus conductor replied politely 'Well madam, you should have rung the bell.'
'Nonsense', said the woman rudely, 'I've got a bad back and couldn't ring the bell.'
'Well', said the conductor, 'Quasimodo had a bad back and he managed it.'

What do Aliens call saucepans?
Unidentified frying objects.

MAN: Would you two stop fighting – you're driving me crazy.
KIDS: OK – we'll stop the car and let you get out!

Why is there such a disaster when a waiter drops a platter of turkey?
Because it's the fall of Turkey, the outbreak of China and the eruption of Greece.

A man walked into a pub with a newt on his shoulder. He went up to the barman and said, 'Can I have a pint of beer for myself and a glass of water for my newt, Tiny?'
The barman gave him his beer and was just about to give the glass of water to the newt when he turned to the man and said, 'Why do you call your newt Tiny?' And the man answered 'Because he's my newt.'

'Doctor, Doctor, I feel like a billiard ball.'
'Stop pushing in, and get to the end of the queue.'

'Would you sign this petition?'
'Against what?'
'Use my back if you want.'

Will the train standing on platform 7 please get back on to the rails.

What did Cinderella say when her photos were delayed at the chemist?
Some day my 'prints' will come.

Where does Tarzan buy his clothes?
At 'jungle' sales.

SHERLOCK HOLMES:	Ah Watson, I see that you are wearing your winter underwear.
WATSON:	Amazing Holmes, how did you deduce that?
HOLMES:	Elementary my dear Watson, you forgot to put your trousers on.

An Alien came down from Mars and was longing
for a drink. He walked across the street, into a pub,
and said to the barman, 'Please serve me a drink.'
The barman was shocked, never having seen an
Alien before, and the following conversation took
place:

BARMAN: Sorry mate, but it's the house rules, I
can't serve Aliens.

ALIEN: Well, if I buy all the people in this pub
a drink, then will you serve me?

BARMAN: Listen, my little green friend, I *don't*
serve Aliens.

ALIEN: OK – I'll buy you, everybody in the
pub and everybody in England a
drink, then will you serve me?

BARMAN: No Alien, I won't, now please leave
the pub.

ALIEN: Mr Barman, there is no need to be
rude – I will buy you a drink, everyone
in the pub, everyone in England and
even Europe as well – now will you
serve me?

BARMAN: No – now shove off.

ALIEN: You drive a very hard bargain – I will
buy the people in the pub a drink,
plus the whole of England, Europe
and everyone in the world. Now will
you give me a drink?

BARMAN: No Alien, I won't.

ALIEN: OK, OK, let's not be silly. My final
offer – I will buy a drink for everyone
in this pub, the whole of England,
Europe, the world, and on top of that
– the universe – now will you serve
me?

BARMAN: Well, OK then.
ALIEN: Good. Now, have you got change for a ZONK?

Where do ghosts go to eat?
To a 'Resta-haunt'.

BOY: Dad, I don't want a BMX for Christmas.
DAD: Why not, son?
BOY: Because I found one in the wardrobe.

What do you do when you meet twin witches?
Nothing, because you can't tell which witch is which.

What occurs once in every minute, twice in every moment but not once in five thousand years?
The letter M.

Why are airline passengers so polite to each other?
They don't want to fall out.

Did you hear about the two flies playing football in the saucer?
They were practising for the cup.

Why is the sky so high?
So the birds won't bang their heads.

If Ching Chong went to Hong Kong to play ping pong and died, what would they put on his coffin?
A lid.

Why did Silly Billy get into trouble for feeding the monkeys at the zoo?
He fed them to the lions.

A countryman was walking through the centre of his nearest town where he read a sign outside a builder's merchant.
CAST IRON SINKS – it said.
'Well aren't city folk stupid', he said, 'everyone knows that.'

Why didn't the man take a bus home from work?
Because his wife would have made him take it back.

Why do giraffes have such long necks?
Because they can't stand the smell of their feet.

In a school, the geniuses were on the 1st floor, the clever people were on the 2nd floor, the dull people on the 3rd floor and the really thick people were on the 4th floor. What do you think was on the 5th floor?
The Staffroom.

HISTORY TEACHER: Maria, in the Second World War, the Germans conquered France, then they conquered Belgium, Holland, Denmark and several other countries. Why do you think they didn't conquer Britain?

MARIA: I know miss, they ran out of conkers.

How did the dachshund die?
He was walking round a tree when he met his end.

Who wears the largest shoes in the world?
The person with the largest feet.

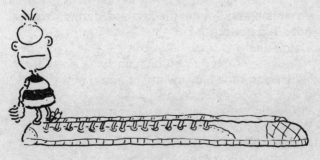

Have you heard about the man who managed to combine a retriever and a tortoise?
He sends it to the shops and it comes back with last week's paper.

What keeps jazz musicians on earth?
Groovity!

A man fell out of a plane.
Unfortunately his parachute didn't work.
Fortunately there was a haystack below.
Unfortunately there was a pitchfork in it.
Fortunately he missed the pitchfork.
Unfortunately he missed the haystack too.

What is black, lives in the sea and shouts, 'You've got a big bottom'?
Crude oil.

Why wasn't the lady swimmer afraid of the shark?
It was a man-eating shark.

What goes OOM OOM and gives milk?
A cow walking backwards.

1st BOY:	What is frozen water?
2nd BOY:	Iced water.
1st BOY:	What is frozen cream?
2nd BOY:	Iced cream.
1st BOY:	What is frozen ink?
2nd BOY:	Iced ink.
1st BOY:	Well go and have a bath then.

Did you hear about the new Dracula doll?
You wind it up and it bites a Barbie doll in the neck.

What did Adam say the day before Christmas?
It's Christmas, Eve.

What do you give to someone who has everything?
Penicillin.

JUDGE:	You have a choice, thirty days or £100.
DEFENDANT:	I'll take the money.

What did one eye say to the other eye?
Between you and me, something smells.

My Mum wanted a fur coat for Christmas so my Dad bought her a donkey jacket.

Did you hear about the man who bought a microwave bed and got eight hours sleep in four minutes?

Gypsy to her husband, 'Give me your hand, I feel like reading something before I go to sleep.'

GORDON'S GIGGLERS!

Why does Gordon the Gopher squeak?
Because he doesn't know the words. (squeak, squeak)

When will Gordon be the hunkiest guy in Great Britain?
When everyone in Great Britain has emigrated.

What's yellow and turns red at the touch of a button?
Gopher in a liquidizer. (ugh)

How do you recognise a hippy Gopher?
Flared sneakers.

What's furry and can't keep still?
A Gopher in a tumble dryer.

TEACHER: Why were you off yesterday, Gordon?
GORDON: Because I was sick.
TEACHER: Sick of what?
GORDON: Sick of school.

Why has a Gopher got two feet?
Because he would look funny with six inches.

Know how Gordon doubles his money?
He tears it in two.

What's yellow, green and slimy?
A Gopher in a swamp.

What do you call a Gopher with bananas in his ears?
Anything you like – he can't hear you.

Gordon's friend is called Glug Glug Glug, because the vicar fell into the font.

Why did Gordon cross the road?
To prove he wasn't a chicken.

What's funny about a Gopher's leg?
The bottom is at the top.

What's small, hairy and has got red spots?
A Gopher with measles.

Where was Gordon when the lights went out?
In the dark.

How does an old Gopher avoid falling hair?
He gets out of the way.

A stupid Gopher had two horses in a field and wanted to be able to tell the difference between them.

First he tried plaiting their tails, but the plaits came undone. So he tried painting them different colours, but the paint came off.

Then Gordon came by and said, 'I know how we can tell them apart – the black one is bigger than the white one.'

How does Gordon hide when he doesn't want to eat his lunch?
Paints the soles of his feet green, and floats upside down in a bowl of pea soup.

How does Gordon hide when he doesn't want to eat his tea?
Paints the soles of his feet red, and dives into the strawberry jam.

What do you call a Gopher with five ears, three mouths, three noses and seven eyes?
UGLY.

What is hairy, ugly and blue?
A Gopher holding its breath.

What did Gordon say to his girlfriend?
Let's 'Gopher' a walk.

What kind of umbrella does Gordon use on a rainy day?
A wet one.

What goes squeak, squeak, squeak *plop*?
Gordon laughing his head off.

Last summer Gordon stayed in a small village by the sea and his landlady kept animals.
On the first day one of her chickens died so he had chicken for dinner.
On the second day one of her pigs died so he had pork chops for dinner.
On the third day one of her ducks died so he had roast duck for dinner.
On the fourth day her husband died so he left before dinner!

Why did Gordon put his bed in the fire?
Because he wanted to sleep like a log.

TEACHER: If you had £7.50 in one pocket and £3.80 in the other pocket, what would you have?
GORDON: Phillip's trousers, miss.

A man went into a second-hand shop to get a brain.
The lady behind the counter said there were three brains for sale.
The first brain was Phillip Schofield's and was £25 000, the second was Sarah Greene's and that was £50 000, but the brain-of-the-week was Gordon's and that was £100 000. 'Why', asked the man, 'is Gordon's brain so much more expensive than Phillip's or Sarah's? 'Ah', said the shop assistant, 'Gordon's hasn't been used.'

Gordon says (and he should know), 'Better to keep one's mouth shut and be thought an idiot than to open it and have it proved beyond doubt'.

Why does Gordon the Gopher keep biscuits in his comic?
Because he likes crumby jokes.

Why does Gordon call his dog Camera?
Because it's always snapping.

What did Phillip say when Gordon ran up the beanstalk?
He's been and gone and done a runner.

Why did Gordon bring a car to the *Going Live!* studio?
To drive Sarah and Phillip up the wall.

Did you know that last Saturday Gordon sat up all night wondering where the sun had gone?
Next morning it dawned on him.

Why does Gordon the Gopher smile every time there is a flash of lightning?
Because he thinks that he is having his photograph taken.

And now a word from Gordon for all those born this week.
Coochy coochy coo.

It it takes half a yard of buttermilk to make a waistcoat for a duck. How long does it take a Gopher in ballet shoes to crawl through the Double Dare gunge tank?
Are you stuck? – So is Gopher!

What do you call a Gopher with seventeen GCSEs?
A liar.

FAVOURITE JOKES FROM THE STARS
(So this is what makes them laugh!)

Aztec Camera
A man went into a shop and asked for a wasp.
'I'm sorry sir, we don't sell wasps', replied the shopkeeper.
'Then why are there two in your window?' enquired the customer.

Two from **A-Ha**
What do you call a fish with no eye?
FSH (No 'I').

What do you call a deer with no ear?
'D'.

Mental As Anything
What's green with check trousers?
Rupert the snooker table.

Europe
Why did the skunk take a painkiller?
Because he had a stinking headache.

Alexander O'Neil
What does a snooker ball do when it stops rolling?
It looks round.

Andrew Ridgeley
What do you get hanging from monkey puzzle trees?
Very sore arms.

George Michael
Did you hear about the girl who was named after
her mother?
They called her Mum.

Two from the **Proclaimers**
PUNK IN BOUTIQUE: I want to try on those
slashed jeans in the
window.
SALES ASSISTANT: This is a respectable shop –
you'll have to try them on
in the fitting room like
everyone else.

What did the ghost teacher say to her pupils?
*Watch the board – I'll go through it just once
more.*

Prefab Sprout
MAN: Please call your dog off.
LITTLE GIRL: I don't want to call him OFF – I like
calling him Rover.

Three from **Bros**
What's pink and stands in the corner?
A naughty pig.

Why can't a woman with a wooden leg change a
£1 note?
Because she's only got 'half a knicker'.

'Doctor, Doctor, I keep seeing Mickey Mouse.'
'Don't worry, you're just having a ''Disney'' spell.'

T'Pau
What do you call a snowman in the desert?
A puddle.

The Madness
Why do you have to go to the fish and chip shop?
Well, the fish and chip shop won't come to you.

Patsy Kensit
What's got eight wheels and flies?
A council dustcart.

Dollar
What's small, white and makes your eyes water
when it giggles?
A tickled onion.

Billy Idol
A man went into a cafe and asked for a cup of tea
and a packet of helicopter crisps.
'Here's your tea sir', said the cafe owner, 'But I'm
afraid we haven't any helicopter crisps – *we've
only got ''PLANE''.'*

Erasure

LITTLE GIRL CRYING:	Boo hoo, I've lost my pussycat.
HELPFUL LADY:	Don't cry little girl, why don't you ask your mummy to put a 'lost' notice in the window?
LITTLE GIRL:	That's no good, my pussycat can't read.

Two from **Deacon Blue**

Did you hear about the witch who was top of her class?
She was the best speller.

Do you know what happened to the burglar who fell into the cement mixer?
He became a hardened criminal.

Bonnie Tyler

What's a duck's favourite TV programme?
The feather forecast.

Alison Moyet

Why did the ant run along the top of the biscuit packet?
Because the instructions said, 'Tear along the dotted line'.

Climie Fisher

POLICEMAN TO PEDESTRIAN: Just a moment sir, why are you trying to cross the road at this highly dangerous point? If you just take a few steps up the road you'll see a zebra crossing.

IRATE PEDESTRIAN: Well, I hope he's having more luck than I am.

Terence Trent D'Arby

Why did the old man have jelly in one ear and some jam sponge in the other?
Because he was a TRIFLE deaf.

JUST JOKIN'

At an airline ticket desk a little boy standing
between his mother and father told the desk clerk
he was only two years old. The clerk was very
suspicious and said to the child, 'Do you know
what happens to little boys who lie?'
'Yes', said the boy, 'they fly half-price.'

TEACHER: Justin, give me the present tense of
           the verb 'to walk'.
JUSTIN: Um I walk . . . um you walk . . . um he
           walks.
TEACHER: Quicker please.
JUSTIN: I run, you run, he runs.

ZOO ATTENDANT: There's no need to be afraid
                 of that lion – he was brought
                 up on a bottle.
VISITOR: So was I, but I like steak and
                 chips now.

An old lady was riding a motorbike and knitting at
the same time.
A policeman drove up beside her and shouted at
her to 'pull over'.
'No', she said, 'socks'.

'Mummy, Mummy, John's broken my doll.'
'How did that happen?'
It cracked when I hit him with it.

What did the boy octopus say to the girl octopus?
I wanna hold your hand, hand, hand, hand.

What do monsters most like watching on TV?
BeastEnders.

Why can't Cinderella play hockey?
Because she keeps running away from the ball.

Why did the kangaroo scold her children?
Because they ate biscuits in bed.

How do you find a lost rabbit?
Make a noise like a nice fresh carrot.

Why do we plant bulbs?
So the worms can see where they are going.

ANIMAL LOVER: Mum, can I keep a skunk under my bed?
MOTHER: What about the smell?
ANIMAL LOVER: He'll get used to it.

'Doctor, Doctor I think I'm a puppy dog.'
'Well, lie on the couch and I'll examine you.'
'I can't, I'm not allowed on the furniture.'

DOCTOR: You need glasses.
PATIENT: That's brilliant – how did you know?
DOCTOR: I could tell as soon as you walked
           through the window.

'Doctor, Doctor, I feel like a window frame.'
'Are you in pain?'
'No Doctor, that's the trouble, the panes in ME.'

'Doctor, Doctor, my family thinks I'm mad.'
'Why is that?'
'Because I like sausages.'
'There's nothing strange about that – I like
sausages too.'
*'Really, how wonderful – you must come and see
my collection, I've got thousands.'*

How many yuppies does it take to change a light
bulb?
*Two. One to find the Filofax and one to phone
the electrician.*

41

Who went into the lion's den with his eyes closed, and came out alive?
The lion.

MOLLY: What shall we play?
ROSIE   Let's play schools.
MOLLY: OK – but let's play I'm absent.

Mummy crab, Daddy crab and Baby crab went for a picnic. Whilst Daddy and Baby crab were swimming, Mummy crab became hungry and ate half the picnic. Daddy crab then returned and he was hungry too, so he ate the rest of the picnic. When Baby crab came back he opened the picnic basket and asked where all the food had gone.
'Daddy crab and I have eaten it all,' said Mummy crab.
'Well,' said Baby crab, 'I think you're both SHELLFISH.'

What do you call a book that tells fleas how to find chocolate?
The Itch-Hikers Guide to the Galaxy.

What did the Big Chief Running Water call his two sons?
Hot and Cold.

What did Big Chief Running Water call his third son?
Little Drip.

If all the school boys who fell asleep in class were laid end to end – they'd be much more comfortable.

What do you call a robbery in Peking?
A Chinese take-away.

1st FARMER: Why has your pig got a wooden leg?
2nd FARMER: It's a great pig – it saved my life.
1st FARMER: How?
2nd FARMER: The farm caught fire and it rang the fire brigade.
1st FARMER: That doesn't explain why it's got a wooden leg.
2nd FARMER: Well you don't think I'd eat such a great pig all at once, do you?

What sits in a pram and wobbles?
A jelly baby.

A man went into a butcher's shop and said:
'What have you got today?'
'Well sir, we have budgerigar or venison, what would you like?'
'What do you recommend?'
'Well that depends on whether you want something cheap or something dear.'

'Waiter, waiter, this lobster's only got one claw.'
'It's been in a fight sir.'
'Then bring me the winner.'

There once was a man from Bengal
Who went to a fancy dress ball,
He went just for fun
Dressed up as a bun
And the dog ate him up in the hall.

What's black, white, black, white, black, white?
A nun rolling down a hill.

What's black and white and laughing?
The nun that pushed her.

BABY SNAKE: Mum, are we poisonous?
MOTHER SNAKE: Yes, we are, why dear?
BABY SNAKE: I've just bit my lip.

Did you hear about the vegetarian cannibal who
would only eat 'swedes'?

What are hail stones?
Hard-boiled rain.

There was a hearse on its way to the cemetery one cold and icy day. It was travelling up a steep hill when the rear door opened and the coffin slid out and began to roll down the hill. Half-way down, the corpse jumped out and ran into a chemist's shop shouting, 'Have you got something to stop me coffin?'

A duck went into a shop one day and asked for a pound of apples.
'That will be 95p,' said the assistant.
'Put it on the bill,' said the duck.

Why can't you fool a snake?
Because he hasn't got a leg to pull.

POLICEMAN:	I'm going to have to ask you to accompany me to the station.
MAN:	Why – what have I done?
POLICEMAN:	Nothing – it's just that I'm frightened to go on my own.

Who invented fractions?
Henry the 1/8th.

There was a boy called Oliver Mickey Smith and he went to school for the first time.
The teacher began the morning by reading out the register and when she came to Oliver's name she called out 'Oliver Smith'.
'Please miss,' said Oliver, 'my dad doesn't like people taking the mickey out of my name'.

There was an old man from Peru
Whose limericks stopped at line two . . .

Why do bees strike?
For shorter flowers and more honey.

What do you get if you cross a centipede and a
parrot?
A walkie-talkie.

What is a myth?
A female moth.

A sailor on a transatlantic liner was a very keen
conjuror. He had a parrot who knew all the tricks,
but, unfortunately, whenever he performed a trick,
the parrot would shout, 'Phoney, phoney, it's up
his sleeve.' One day the ship struck an iceberg and
sank. The parrot and the conjuror survived, and
for three days they clung to a piece of wood
without saying a word. Finally the parrot looked at
the sailor suspiciously and said, 'OK wise guy,
what did you do with the ship?'

What is a tornado?
Mother nature doing the twist.

MUM: I've just looked in the mirror and I've got
         two grey hairs.
EMMA: Why's that Mummy?
MUM: (seizing the chance) Because you're such
         a bad girl to me, I expect.
EMMA: Gosh Mummy, you must have been
         awful to Grandma.

'Doctor, Doctor, I've just swallowed the film from
my camera.'
'Well we'll just have to see if anything develops.'

1st FATHER: Can your daughter spell her name?
2nd FATHER: Yes, forwards and backwards. And
              she's only four.
1st FATHER: Amazing. What's her name?
2nd FATHER: Anna.

What would happen if Nigel Lawson had a leak in
his bath?
*Mrs Thatcher would live in No 10 DROWNING
STREET.*

A young vet owed his friend some money but as
he was very hard-up he didn't know how he was
going to pay him – then he had an idea. He went
to the aquarium at the back of his surgery and
removed a pathetic creature from the bottom. He
placed it in a jam jar with some water and some
food and sent it round to his friend with a note –
HERE IS THE SICK SQUID I OWE YOU.

There was a young man from Leeds
Who swallowed a packet of seeds,
Within just one hour
His nose was a flower
And his head was a riot of weeds.

A teacher had ten very lazy children in her class, so she decided to trick them into doing some work.
'I've got a very easy test here for the laziest pupil in the class', she said, 'I'd like the laziest pupil to put up their hand.'
Nine hands went up.
'Why didn't you put your hand up?' she asked the tenth pupil.
'Too much trouble,' was the reply.

Why does a banana skin on the pavement remind you of music?
Because if you don't C sharp you'll B flat on your back.

How do you get a baby astronaut to sleep?
You rock-et.

Why was the strawberry crying?
Because its mother was in a jam.

Why do birds have feathers?
Because they'd look silly in plastic macs.

BOY: Mum I think my teacher is madly in love with me.
MUM: What on earth makes you think that, darling?
BOY: She's always putting kisses all over my sums.

What do you get if you cross a wireless with a clock?
The Radio Times.

Why is honey scarce in Bolivia?
Because there is only one 'B' in it.

A man taught his dog to speak English, and took it for a walk in the meadow. The dog turned to a cow who was quietly munching the grass and said: 'How now brown cow?'
The cow was so surprised that he gave the dog a 'pat' on the head.

What time of the day was Adam born?
A little before Eve.

Why do dragons sleep during the day?
So that they can fight KNIGHTS.

STEPHEN: But why have I got to go to school? Nobody likes me, I haven't got any friends . . .

MOTHER: But darling, you're the headmaster.

What did the two sardines say when they met in a tin?
Long time no sea.

What is the longest word in the English language?
SMILES – because there's a 'MILE' between the first and last letter.

A thunderstorm was raging over Britain one night and little Tracey woke up in fright and ran to her parents' bedroom.
'Daddy', she cried, 'why is it thundering?'
'Well, every time someone tells a really big lie, Heaven gets very angry and so it thunders'.
'But Daddy,' said Tracey, 'isn't everyone asleep at this time of night?'
'Well yes', said her father, 'but this is about the time when newspapers are printed'.

What do you call an overweight ghost who haunts the opera house?
FAT-TUM of the Opera.

Three tomatoes walking along the road; Mummy tomato, Daddy tomato and Baby tomato. Baby tomato was dragging behind because he only had small legs so Daddy tomato turns round to Baby tomato and says, 'KETCH-UP'.

MUM: I'll put the washing machine on.
LITTLE BOY: Don't be silly mum, it won't suit you.

A dragon arrived at Dr Frankenstein's surgery looking very ill.
'What's the matter?' asked the doctor.
'I have a terrible stomach ache', explained the dragon.
'What have you eaten in the last few hours?' enquired the doctor.
'Only a knight in shining armour', said the dragon.
'Did he smell quite fresh when you took him out of his armour?' asked Dr Frankenstein.
'Oh,' said the dragon, 'I didn't know I was supposed to take him out of his armour'.

What would you call a three-foot disc jockey?
A compact disc player.

Did you hear about the boat loaded with yo-yos which hit a rock?
It sank seventy-six times.

A large gorilla walked down the high street and fancied a cup of tea, so he popped into a café and ordered a cup. The waitress, scared to death, asked the café owner what she should do. 'Keep him talking while I phone the police.' The waitress nervously poured him a cup of tea and the gorilla pulled a £1 coin from behind his ear. Not being proud, the waitress saw a chance to make some money and gave the gorilla 5p change. Then she remembered the café owner's advice and stammered, 'Actually we don't get many gorillas in here.' 'Not surprising at 95p a cup', replied the gorilla.

SOME 'KNOCK KNOCK' JOKES

KNOCK KNOCK
Who's there?
Gustave
Gustave who?
Gustave wind, draughty isn't it?

KNOCK KNOCK
Who's there?
Shirley
Shirley who?
Shirley you know me?

KNOCK KNOCK
Who's there?
Asif
Asif who?
Asif you don't know.

KNOCK KNOCK
Who's there?
Asiya
Asiya who?
Asiya tomorrow, since you don't recognise me today.

KNOCK KNOCK
Who's there?
Opportunity
It can't be.
Why not?
Opportunity never knocks twice.

KNOCK KNOCK
Who's there?
July
July who?
July in bed all morning?

KNOCK KNOCK
Who's there?
Sue
Sue who?
Sue prized to see you.

KNOCK KNOCK
Who's there?
Granny

KNOCK KNOCK
Who's there?
Granny

KNOCK KNOCK
Who's there?
Granny

KNOCK KNOCK
Who's there?
Auntie
Auntie who?
Aren't you glad Granny's gone?

KNOCK KNOCK
Who's there?
Phillip
Phillip who?
Phillip my glass.

KNOCK KNOCK
Who's there?
Cows
Cows who?
Cows don't go who, cows go moo.

KNOCK KNOCK
Who's there?
Moyra
Moyra who?
Moyra see you, Moyra like you.

KNOCK KNOCK
Who's there?
Avenue
Avenue who?
Avenue been waiting a long time?

KNOCK KNOCK
Who's there?
Kellogg's
Kellogg's who?
It's a cereal, I'll tell you next week.

KNOCK KNOCK
Who's there?
Dawn
Dawn who?
Dawn leave me standing out in the cold.

KNOCK KNOCK
Who's there?
Havelock
Havelock who?
Havelock and you'll see who's there.

KNOCK KNOCK
Who's there?
Owen
Owen who?
Owen will you open the door?

KNOCK KNOCK
Who's there?
Marcella
Marcella who?
Marcella full of water, can I borrow a bucket?

KNOCK KNOCK
Who's there?
Bernadette
Bernadette who?
Bernadette my dinner and I'm starving.

KNOCK KNOCK
Who's there?
Alf
Alf who?
Alf find out later.

KNOCK KNOCK
Who's there?
Owl
Owl who?
Owl you know unless you open the door.

KNOCK KNOCK
Who's there?
Mike
Mike who?
Mike car won't start.

KNOCK KNOCK
Who's there?
Wilma
Wilma who?
Wilma supper be ready soon?

KNOCK KNOCK
Who's there?
Godfrey
Godfrey who?
Godfrey tickets for a Michael Jackson concert.

KNOCK KNOCK
Who's there?
Sultan
Sultan who?
Sultan Pepper.

KNOCK KNOCK
Who's there?
Worzel
Worzel who?
Upstairs, first on the right.

KNOCK KNOCK
Who's there?
Yamaha
Yamaha who?
Yamaha wants you to go home.

KNOCK KNOCK
Who's there?
Wooden shoe
Wooden shoe who?
Wooden shoe like to know?

KNOCK KNOCK
Who's there?
Alison
Alison who?
Alison to my radio in the morning.

KNOCK KNOCK
Who's there?
Howard
Howard who?
Howard you like to think of an ending yourself?

YOUR MOTHER WOULDN'T LIKE IT

Why did the cannibal return from his holidays with only one leg?
He went self-catering.

Why are sausages bad mannered?
Because they spit in the fying pan.

Willie with a taste for gore
Nailed his sister to the door,
Mother said with humour quaint
Willie dear, don't spoil the paint.

What do you give a seasick elephant?
Lots of room.

LADY: My dog is so idle.
FRIEND: Why's that?
LADY: Well I was watering the garden the other day and he wouldn't even lift up his leg to help.

What makes antifreeze?
Hide her nightie!

What do boys do standing up and dogs do with one leg in the air?
Shake hands.

Why are adults boring?
Because they are 'groan-ups'.

Why was the sand wet?
Because the sea weed.

Why couldn't Batman go fishing?
Because Robin kept eating all the worms.

What do you call two robbers?
A pair of knickers.

What did the policeman say when he saw a
lavatory in the middle of the road?
A loo, a loo, a loo.

What do you get if you cross a tin of baked beans
and an onion?
Tear gas.

What do you call a septic cat?
Puss.

Why does the ocean roar?
*Well so would you if you had crabs on your
bottom.*

CHILD: But Mummy, I don't want to go to
           France.
MOTHER: Shut up and keep swimming.

What do you get if you sit under a cow?
A pat on the head.

What happened to the girl who slept with her head
under the pillow?
The fairies took all her teeth away.

What happens at a cannibal wedding?
Everyone toasts the bride.

Did you hear about the dentist that became a brain
surgeon?
His drill slipped.

What's yellow, brown and hairy?
Cheese on toast, dropped on the carpet.

What's the best thing to do if you nose goes on strike?
Pick-it.

BOY: Where are you going Mum?

MUM: To the doctor. I don't like the look of your sister.

BOY: I'll come with you, I don't like the look of her either.

Daddy, there's a man at the door collecting for the old people's home – shall I give him Grandpa?

What do you call a dog with four broken legs?
Anything you like – it won't come.

There was a man in the pub who only had one arm and he was trailing his empty sleeve in another man's drink.
'You're trailing your sleeve in my drink.'
'That's all right, there ain't no ARM in it.'

What's your son going to be when he passes all his exams?
An old-age-pensioner.

What's worse than fitting ten men into one dustbin?
Fitting one man into ten dustbins.

TEACHER: Charles, what is a cannibal?
CHARLES: I don't know miss.
TEACHER: Well what would you be if you ate your Mummy and your Daddy?
CHARLES: An orphan, miss.

What goes PECK, PECK, PECK, PECK BANG?
A chicken in a minefield.

What has two legs, one wheel and flies?
A wheelbarrow full of manure.

Two snails were walking down a path followed by
a slug. Mummy snail turned to Daddy snail and
said, 'Isn't it lucky Baby snail isn't with us, because
we're being followed by a streaker.'

'How did you get that puncture?'
'Ran over a milk bottle.'
'Didn't you see it?
'No, the silly man had it under his coat!'

In the reading room of a library a man was
reading the birth and death statistics. Suddenly he
turned to the man sitting next to him and
whispered, 'Do you know every time I breathe a
man dies?'
'Well, why don't you try using a mouthwash?'
replied the stranger.

'But Henry, that isn't our baby!'
'Shut up, it's a better pram.'

A little boy looks over the next-door neighbour's
fence and says, 'Please can I have my arrow back?'
'Certainly, where is it?'
'In the side of your cat.'

ELEPHANTS, FROGS AND COWS

What's purple, has four legs and stands in the middle of a field jogging?
A cow in a track suit.

'Waiter, have you got frogs legs?'
'No, it's just the way I walk!'

What's very big and mutters?
A mumbo-jumbo.

Why did the elephant walk on two legs?
To give the ants a better chance.

How do you shoot a pink elephant?
With a pink elephant gun.

How do you shoot a white elephant?
Paint it pink, then shoot it.

What did the grape say when the elephant stepped on it?
Nothing, it just gave a little wine.

What do you get if a herd of elephants tramples on Batman and Robin?
Flatman and Ribbon.

Why did the cow give away her bucket of milk?
Because she had 'an-udder'.

Why do elephants have big ears?
Because Noddy wouldn't pay the ransom.

When do elephants have sixteen legs?
When there are four of them.

What have elephants and frogs got in common?
They can't drive tractors.

There were two cows in a field, which one was going on holiday?
The one with the wee calf.

What do you get if you cross a herd of cows with a panic situation?
Udder chaos.

Why can't an elephant ride a bike?
Because he hasn't a thumb to ring the bell.

Why do elephants wear sandals?
So they won't sink into the sand.

Why do ostriches stick their heads in the sand?
To see the elephants that don't wear sandals.

What do you call a girl with a frog on her head?
Lily.

How long should an elephant's leg be?
Long enough to touch the ground.

What do you get if you cross an elephant with a swallow?
Lots of broken telegraph poles.

What happens when a frog parks his car on a double yellow line?
It gets 'toad' away.

What should you do if a cow decides to sleep in your bed?
Find somewhere else to sleep.

What do you get when you cross an elephant with a goldfish?
Swimming trunks.

What is large and heavy and grey and found at the North Pole?
A lost elephant.

Why is an elephant large, grey and wrinkled?
Because if it was small, white and round it would be an aspirin.

No seriously, why are elephants grey and wrinkled?
Because they are so hard to iron.

Why did the cow fall out of the tree?
Because it was dead.

What is a frog's favourite flower?
A croakus.

Why do elephants wear pink tennis shoes?
Because white ones show the dirt.

Why do elephants have swollen ankles?
Because their pink tennis shoes are too tight.

Why shouldn't you go into the jungle at midday?
Because that's when elephants do their parachute practice.

Why are crocodiles flat?
Because they went into the jungle at midday.

What did Tarzan say when he saw a herd of elephants coming towards him?
Oh look, there's a herd of elephants.

What did Tarzan say when he saw a herd of elephants coming towards him wearing sun-glasses?
Nothing – he didn't recognise them.

An Englishman, an Irishman and a Scotsman were walking down the street when they saw a cow. The Englishman said, 'Oh look, there's my cow', and the other two chaps said, 'Prove it'. Well he couldn't and the Irishman said, 'That isn't your cow, that's my cow'. Again, the other chaps said 'Prove it', and of course he couldn't. Finally the Scotsman said, 'That's my cow and I can prove it. Just look, it's got bagpipes underneath.'

FINAL FUNNIES

A boxer collected ties. He had so many that he
needed names for all of them so he wouldn't get
them mixed up. He had a FRANK tie, a STEVE tie
and so on.
One day his son was going to a friend's birthday
party and wanted to borrow a tie. His Dad went to
the closet and took out a white one.
'Here,' said Dad, 'have this one but take good
care of it, it's my MIKE TIE SON'.

What's the definition of an archaeologist?
A man whose career is in ruins.

Why did the parrot wear a raincoat?
He wanted to be POLY-UN-SATURATED.

Dr Jones had just completed his 2000th successful operation.
As he washed his hands a young student doctor asked how he had accomplished such a remarkable record. 'Ah well', said the surgeon, 'it took an awful lot of patients'.

1st SCHOOLGIRL: I think they should introduce a four day week for schoolchildren.
2nd SCHOOLGIRL: I agree, they should abolish Monday, Tuesday and Wednesday.

What do you get if you cross a hedgehog and a giraffe?
A toothbrush.

A man was walking past the Post Office Tower. He looked up and saw two men jump off and fly round, and then land back on top of the Tower. The man wanted to know how they did it, so he ran to the top of the Tower and asked them.
'Oh it's easy', said one of the men, 'all you do is jump and flap your arms'.
So the man jumped off, flapped his arms and fell all the way down to the pavement below, where, as you can imagine, he made rather a mess. The two men were watching from the top of the Tower and one turned to the other and said, 'You know for an Archangel, Gabriel, you've got a very odd sense of humour'.

Why does Santa wear red trousers?
Because his blue ones are at the cleaners.

What was the first smoke signal the Indians sent?
Help – my blanket's on fire!

TEACHER ON PHONE: You say Samantha has a
sore throat and can't
come to school today. To
whom am I speaking?

PUPIL ON PHONE: This is my mother.

'Doctor, Doctor, I think I'm a bottomless bin.'
'Don't talk rubbish.'

What do you get if you cross a rabbit with a
cockroach?
Bugs bunny.

CUSTOMER:	The crockery in this restaurant must be very clean.
WAITER:	Thank you sir, how did you know?
CUSTOMER:	Well everything tastes of washing-up liquid.

How do you stop a dog digging up the garden?
Hide the spade.

An ant, a grasshopper and a centipede decided to meet at the ant's house. The grasshopper and the ant waited more than an hour for the centipede. Finally he appeared, bathed in sweat.
'Whatever kept you so long?' asked the grasshopper.
'Well, there's a sign outside saying WIPE YOUR FEET', replied the exhausted centipede.

What do you do with a vampire bat?
Play vampire ball.

How do you get rid of water on the knee?
Wear drainpipe trousers.

What did the electrician's children say when he came home late?
Wire you insulate?

| LITTLE BOY BLUE: | Ba ba black sheep have you any wool? |
| SHEEP: | What do you think this is, silly boy – POLYESTER! |

What goes dot, dot, dash, croak?
Morse toad.

What's big, red and eats rocks?
A big red rockeater.

What's big, red and eats sand?
A big red rockeater on a diet.

What's big, red and eats apples?
A big red rockeater turned vegetarian.

What do you call a pop star with a biscuit on his head?
Lionel Rich Tea.

Which pop star wears a white wig?
Judge Michael.

Which pop star reminds you of Peter Pan?
Paul Young.

Why did the boy keep a scooter by his bed?
He was tired of sleepwalking.

Who thinks up Dracula's jokes?
His crypt writer.

We're grateful to everyone who sent in jokes for the *Joke Box Joke Book*, with special thanks to . . .

Elizabeth Richards from Newton Abbot. Saloni Seth, Slough. S Richards, Portsmouth. Rhian Jones, Blackwood. Kelly Thompson, Letheringset. Avril Bridges, Irvine. Janine Terrill, Barnsley. Emma Barker, Sutton Park, Hull. Emma Dargwell, Fife. Jill Fawcett, Leeds. Tina Azeez, Ilford. Mathew Bartram, Ealing. Ramona Zacharias, Cobham. Karen Smithies, Oldham. Alexander Christodoulatas, Rosshire. Tracey Amott, Ruislip. James Robinson, Rhiwbina. Helen Clews, Halesowen. James McDonald, Winchester. Paul Russell, Ruislip. Steven Bowden, Gunnislake. Mark Ayre, Chertsey. Cameron Scott, Roxburgh. Sharon Paine, Hastings. Waheed Bashir, East Ham. Tracy Floyd, Mitcham. Glen Sanson, East Peckham. Rebecca Birch, Brierly Hill. Tiffany Belcher, Erith. Elizabeth Stankard, Leyland. Emma Watton, Eccleshill. Kelly Sallis, Southwick. Amanda Clarke, Malpas. Sarah Cowlin, Weston-Super-Mare. Jamie Parker, Newnham-on-Severn. Melanie Watley, Bath. Angela Liquorish, Leicester. Sanjia Paul, Littleover. Emma Rickford, Southall. Emma Potter, St Helens. Zoe Paterson, Skelmanthorpe. Caroline Angell, Lymm. D Palmer, Exeter. Shantel Thomas, West Norwood. James Ashman, Canterbury. Nicola Perry, Walsall. Veera Ugargol, Wigan. Julie Pickering, Welford on Avon. Kirewderjit Singh, Reading. Wayne McFadden, Bolton. Patricia John, New Cross. Nicola Boldy, Bradford. Howard Thorpe, Southampton. Sarah Holmes, Coventry. So-Hong Wan, Reading. Loraine Palmer, Wigan.

Ruth Ellison, Cheadle. Joanne Foreshaw, Wigan.
Michael Ritchie, Kirkaldy. R & M Gray, Basildon.
Janine Angove, Penzance. Helen Fitzpatrick,
Chepstow. Stuart Lovell, Camberley. Jason
Houchen, South Stanley. Carole Edwards, Tyne &
Wear. Helen Batty, Horsforth. Karen Burton,
Witney. Gillian Reed, Kettering. C O'Connor,
Halifax. Helen Reed, Rugby. Darren Tait,
Edinburgh. Nicola Daley, Ilkeston. Karen Parfitt,
Billericay. Sarah Cobbe, Helsby. Helen Etheridge,
Liverpool. Angela Collins, Louth. Kenneth Gray,
Skene. Emmett McForley, Co Tyrone. Simon
Hawke, Stevenage. Michelle Fothergill, Reading.
Carol-Ann Stewart, Clarkson. Colin Thompson,
Peckham. Jennifer Meadows, Ullesthorpe.
Catherine Swindlehurst, Rawtenstall. Paul Smith,
Chalfont St Peter. Tracey Hill, Peterborough.
Pauline Wood, Edinburgh. Sarah Mullen, Belfast,
Mollie Baxter, Carnforth. Neil Weatherstone, Blyth.
Laura Haynes, Bletchley. Kirsty O'Donnell,
Richmond. Gabriel Mallon, Co Tyrone. Scott
Dovey, Wittersham. Michael Dunne, Tipperary.
Asif & Asiya Siddiquee, Manchester. Imran Fazal,
Pinner. Gavin P Newman, Sutton Coldfield.
Richard Boxley, Stourbridge. Jane Lafferty,
Lanarkshire. David Winterbottom, Middlesbrough.
Kendra Mealing, Redcar. Georgina Bath, Preston.
Karen Bains, Evington. Anthony Leedham,
Romford. Virewderjit Sing, Reading. Judith Harris,
Selby, Toby Kennedy, Islington. Matthew Cornbill,
Sutton Coldfield. Vicki Clarke, Shanklin. Anna
Bowyer, Saffron Walden. Kathryn Walters,
Loughborough. Claire Shearer, County Hexham.
Karen Lowley, Wem. Linda Poulter, Cambridge.
Stephanie Knight, Old Trafford. Katie Bond,

Lymm. Terence Rooney, Dublin. Denise Witts,
Swindon. Ikbar Bahia, Southall. Angela Preece,
Preston. Nick Doherty, Preston. Katrina MaGuire,
Belfast. Marc Ahmed, Cleveland. Mishka Lockley,
Bury St Edmunds. Louise Hoyle, Clwyd. Karen
Palmer, Harefield. Robert Dalton, Coventry. Louise
Martin, Brighouse. Kelly Tustin, Sindlesham. Zoe
Calvert, Oxford. Clare Hannelly, Heywood. Melanie
Nesbitt, Middlesbrough.